Horrible Histories

DISASTER!

CONTENTS

Watts Books
London • New York • Sydney

FLOOD!

All life on Earth needs water. Most centres of
population are near the sea or a lake or river so
as to have a ready supply of water. But although
water is essential for life it can also be very
dangerous. Stories of catastrophic floods caused
by angry gods are as old as civilisation and
common to cultures all over the world.

Major flood disasters
c. 3500 BC The Great Flood
1219 Norway, lake overflow, 36,000 drowned
1362 Holland, Great Drowning, 30,000 drowned
1421 Failed dykes, Holland, 100,000 drowned
1530 Failed dykes, Holland, 400,000 drowned
1642 River embankments destroyed by rebels,
      Kaifong, China, 300,000 drowned
1876 Storm surge, Ganges and Brahmaputra
      estuaries, India, 200,000 drowned
1887 Hwang Ho, China, 1.5 million drowned
1896 Japan, tidal wave, 27,000 drowned
1931 Hwang Ho river, China, possibly worst
      flood ever. Several millions drowned
1938 Chinese dam destroyed to halt invading
      Japanese, 500,000 Chinese drowned

The Hwang Ho (Yellow River) is called China's Sorrow. Its
banks have been built up 8 metres above the surrounding
plain, where millions of Chinese live. When the banks burst,
as they often do, huge numbers of farms and people are
washed away. During a typical flood, an area of China the
size of Britain is under water.

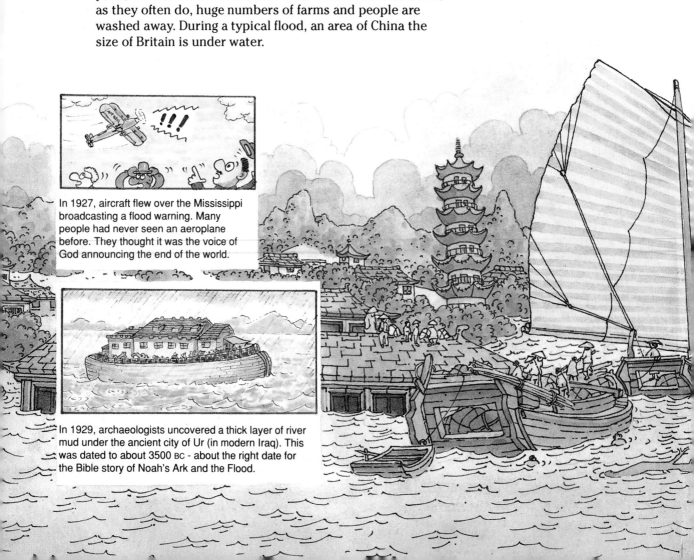

In 1927, aircraft flew over the Mississippi
broadcasting a flood warning. Many
people had never seen an aeroplane
before. They thought it was the voice of
God announcing the end of the world.

In 1929, archaeologists uncovered a thick layer of river
mud under the ancient city of Ur (in modern Iraq). This
was dated to about 3500 BC - about the right date for
the Bible story of Noah's Ark and the Flood.

In 1362, the North Sea flooded Holland. Thirty thousand people were killed. It was called the *Grote Mandrenke* (Great Drowning). Over a million Dutch people have drowned since AD 1000.

The cemetery of Dunwich, Suffolk, was washed away by the sea in 1740. Odd bones, skulls and complete skeletons were washed through the drowned streets of the town.

The River Arno flooded Florence, Italy, in November 1966. Half a million tonnes of mud and slime were deposited in the ancient streets in a single night.

A tsunami, or tidal wave, caused by the Krakatoa volcano in 1883, carried a ship 3 km inland and into the jungle on a nearby island.

One of the oddest floods occurred in Boston, USA, on 15 January 1919. A storage tank containing 4.5 million litres of black treacle burst and sent a huge wave of treacle pouring through the streets. Twenty-one people were killed.

FIRE!

Peking Man was the first human to use fire, about 350,000 years ago. Fire was used for warmth and cooking. Cooking helped to make food safe and edible, and is said to be the greatest hygiene invention of all time. Because fire was once so difficult to produce, villages in the ancient world kept public fires which were never allowed to go out.

Following the earthquake of 1906 in San Francisco a fire was started by someone cooking breakfast. It burned for three days and destroyed 28,000 buildings. Because the earthquake had destroyed the water supply some waiters tried to put out the flames with wine!

The Chicago fire of 1871 is said to have been started by a cow which kicked over an oil lamp. Eighteen thousand buildings were destroyed and two hundred and fifty people were killed.

Emperor Augustus

Emperor Nero

Emperor Augustus started the first Fire Brigade in 27 BC. However, Rome was still destroyed by fire in AD 64. The crazed Emperor Nero is said to have carried on playing his lyre as Rome fell around him.

4

Major fire disasters

97 BC–AD 696	Library of Alexandria destroyed
AD 4	Great Fire of Rome, hundreds burned
1570	Moscow, 200,000 burned
1666	Great Fire of London, 8 died
1769	Brescia, Italy, 300 died
1824	Cairo, 4,000 died
1857	Tokyo, fire after earthquake, 107,000 died
1863	La Campania Church, Chile, 2,500 died
1871	Peshtigo, Wisconsin, forest fire, 1,500 died
1871	Great Fire of Chicago, 250 died
1906	San Francisco, 700 died
1918	Minnesota, forest fire, 800 died
1923	Tokyo, after earthquake, 40,000 died
1934	Hokodate, Japan, 1,500 died
1942	Coconut Grove Club, Boston, 491 died
1983	Great Australian Bushfire, 200,000 sheep and 77 people died

Some fires start naturally. The great Australian bushfire of 1983 devastated an area of about 8,000 sq km. One couple survived the passing firestorm by turning the garden hose on their car and sheltering inside.

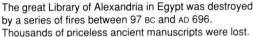

The great Library of Alexandria in Egypt was destroyed by a series of fires between 97 BC and AD 696. Thousands of priceless ancient manuscripts were lost.

An earthquake in Tokyo in 1923 caused winds to whip up the small fires which had started in damaged buildings. Traditional Japanese buildings of that period were built mainly of wood and paper because of the danger of earthquakes. Forty thousand died in the swift flames.

The Great Fire of London started in 1666 in a bakery in Pudding Lane. It raged for three days, destroying most of the city. King Charles II helped with the fire-fighting. Twenty thousand people were made homeless, but only eight died.

People have tried to explain earthquakes in many different ways:

Inuits believed that earthquakes were caused by a giant whale twitching its tail.

Some native Americans believed that a giant tortoise held up the Earth. It sometimes moved.

The Greeks thought that the god Atlas stood on the edge of the world holding up the sky. He occasionally stumbled.

EARTHQUAKE!

The surface of the Earth is covered by a layer of hard rock called the crust. Underneath the crust is a layer of molten rock. The solid crust is not in one piece. It is made up of chunks like pieces of a giant jigsaw puzzle. These chunks are called tectonic plates. They may be thousands of miles across and they float about very slowly on the molten rock below. Earthquakes mainly occur along fault lines where the tectonic plates rub against each other. There may be as many as a million earthquakes every year. Most are too small to be noticed without instruments, but some are immensely powerful. During four thousand years of recorded history, earthquakes are estimated to have caused the deaths of more than seven million people.

The San Andreas Fault runs 450 miles through California. It is one of the most active earthquake areas in the world. In 1906, a major earthquake caused huge destruction and loss of life in San Francisco.

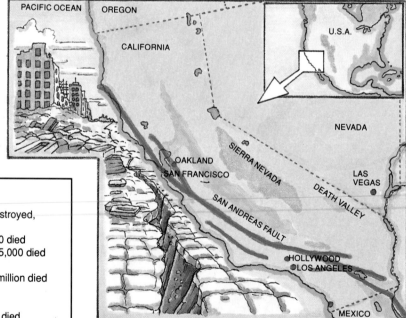

Major earthquake disasters
1450 BC Italy, thousands dead
AD 365 Egypt, Pharos lighthouse destroyed, 50,000 died
  526 Syria, Antioch buried, 250,000 died
  856 Greece, Corinth destroyed, 45,000 died
  893 India, 180,000 died
1202 Eastern Mediterranean, one million died
1556 Shensi, China, 830,000 died
1692 Jamaica, 93,000 died
1703 Edo (Tokyo), Japan, 200,000 died
1755 Lisbon, Portugal, up to 100,000 died
1906 San Francisco, USA, 700 died
1908 Messina, Italy, 160,000 died
1920 Kansu province, China, 180,000 died
1923 Tokyo and Yokahama, Japan, 143,000 died
1964 Alaska, most powerful earthquake recorded
1976 Tangshan province, China, 242,000 died

During the Tokyo earthquake of 1923, a Mrs Chichester-Smith was having a bath in her hotel. The hotel collapsed and she fell to the street in her bath - without a drop of water being spilled.

The power of earthquakes is measured on an instrument called a seismograph according to a scale devised by an American called Charles Richter. The most powerful earthquake ever recorded was the 'Good Friday' earthquake in Alaska in 1964. It measured 8.9 on the Richter scale, and it was equal in power to the explosion of 140 million tonnes of TNT.

In 1755, Lisbon was hit by an earthquake. Sixty thousand people died in the first few minutes of destruction. Waves caused by the earthquake made ships rock free from their moorings one thousand miles away in England.

On the night of 21 June 1990, many Iranians were watching Brazil versus Scotland in a World Cup football match on television. A sudden earthquake killed 40,000 in their beds. There would have been many more deaths if everyone had been asleep.

Some animals, such as dogs and pheasants, are more sensitive to vibrations than humans. They may be warned of an earthquake by tiny vibrations in the ground. The Chinese have become expert at observing animals and can now often predict when an earthquake is going to start.

Huge cracks in the ground appeared during the 1692 earthquake in Jamaica. Many people who fell into the cracks were crushed when they closed up.

An earthquake which struck the Eastern Mediterranean in 1202 may have taken a million lives. In the city of Baalbek, rockfalls killed 200 rhubarb gatherers.

VOLCANOES

The molten rock beneath the Earth's crust sometimes escapes through the crust to the surface. The places where this happens are called volcanoes. Often the molten rock escapes gradually, but sometimes it erupts with immense destructive force.

As many as 300,000 people have been killed by volcanoes since AD 1400.

Major volcano disasters

1500 BC	Santorini caused tidal wave which may have destroyed the Minoan civilisation
477 BC	Italy, Mount Etna, thousands died
AD 79	Italy, Vesuvius destroys Pompeii, 15,000 killed.
150	Tampo Island, New Zealand, probably the greatest eruption in the last 2,000 years
1631	Vesuvius, 18,000 died
1755	Mount Etna again, 36,000 died
1793	Miyi-Yama, Java, 53,000 died
1794	Tungurahua, Ecuador, 40,000 died
1815	Tambora, near Java, 11,994 died
1883	Krakatoa, up to 50,000 died
1902	Mont Pelée, 30,000 died
1985	Nevada del Ruiz, Columbia, mud flow, 23,000 killed

A Roman belief was that Mount Etna in Italy was the prison of the giant Enceladus. His struggles to escape caused eruptions.

The word volcano comes from Vulcan, the blacksmith of the Roman gods. His home was said to be in a volcano in Sicily - called Vulcano.

Mount Vesuvius in Southern Italy erupted in AD 79. The nearby town of Pompeii was buried under millions of tonnes of volcanic ash. Fifteen thousand people died. The ash set hard around their bodies forming a 'mould'. Hundreds of years later after the bodies had rotted away, plaster was poured into some of these almost empty spaces. When the ash was chipped away the plaster casts showed the exact shapes of people in their death agony.

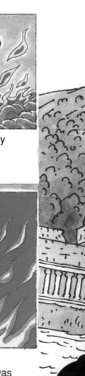

The largest known volcano is Olympus Mons on the planet Mars. It is three times as tall as Mount Everest.

Pneumonoultramicroscopicsilicovolcanoconiosis is the name given to the effects of breathing the poison gas given off by volcanoes.

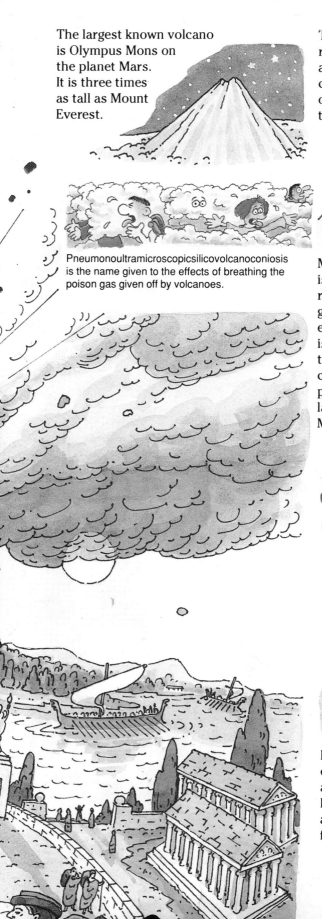

The present Mediterranean island of Santorini is the remains of a previous island called Thera. It exploded in about 1500 BC, causing a tidal wave which destroyed the civilization of the nearby island of Crete. The drowning of Crete is thought by some archaeologists to explain the story of the sunken island of Atlantis.

Mont Pelée on the Caribbean island of Martinique began to rumble in May 1902. The governor failed to order an evacuation. Thirty thousand islanders died. One of the only two survivors was a convict called Auguste Ciparis who was protected by his prison cell. He later toured with a circus as 'The Man who Escaped Hell'.

The Indonesian volcano Tambora exploded violently in 1815. Twelve thousand people were killed by the explosion and 75,000 more died of famine because crops had been destroyed. The strange, gloomy nights are said to have inspired Mary Shelley to write *Frankenstein, or the modern Promethius*, published in 1818.

In 1883, the Indonesian island of Krakatoa suddenly exploded. The rumble was heard up to 3,000 km away. This was possibly the loudest noise ever heard. Fine ash shot 50 km into the upper atmosphere, making the Moon appear blue for many months afterwards.

Hurricane comes from the name of the Arawak Indian god Huracan.

Typhoon comes from the Chinese *tai fung* meaning 'big wind'.

Cyclone comes from the Greek word *kuklos* meaning 'a circle'.

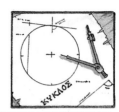

STORM!

Some of the Ancients thought that the wind was the breath of gods. Others believed winds were caused by the flapping wings of god-like eagles on the edge of the world. Now we know that winds are moving air masses powered by the heat of the Sun. The most powerful winds can reach speeds of over 200 mph, or even 400 mph near the centre of tornadoes.

To survive a hurricane, get into a hole or ditch below ground. Avoid open-plan buildings such as swimming pools or sports halls. These sorts of buildings usually suffer the worst wind damage.

In 1780, during the American War of Independence, hurricanes broke up the British, French, Spanish and Dutch fleets. These fleets had sailed to America to attack and re-take the newly independent former colonies.

In 1274, the Chinese Emperor Kublai Khan set out with 1,000 ships to invade Japan, but a typhoon, which the Japanese call the 'Kamikaze' or 'Divine Wind', destroyed his ships and 13,000 men. In 1281, he tried again but another typhoon struck. He lost nearly 4,000 ships and 100,000 soldiers. He gave up.

The biggest storm in British history took place in 1703. Thousands of trees blew down, whole lead roofs of churches flew off, and at least 8,000 lives were lost at sea. Four hundred windmills spun so fast that their sails caught fire.

Major storm disasters
1274 Sea of Japan, typhoon destroys Chinese fleet, 13,000 died
1281 Sea of Japan, typhoon destroys Chinese fleet, 99,997 died
1703 Britain, the Great Storm, over 8,000 died
1737 Bengal, storm and sea surge, 300,000 died
1780 Caribbean hurricanes 25,000 died
1789 India, cyclone caused three huge waves, 300,000 died
1839 Coringa, India, cyclone caused floods, 300,000 died
1876 Backarunge, India, cyclone, 100,000 died
1900 Galveston, USA, 6,000 died
1933-34 Dustbowl storms USA
1959 Japan, 210 kph winds, one million homeless, 5,100 died
1969 Greatest US storm, 320 kph winds, 300 died
1970 Bangladesh cyclone and sea surge, up to 500,000 died
1991 Bangladesh, cyclone and sea surge, ten million homeless, many died

The Dust Bowl storms of 1933-34 in the midwest of the USA caused huge destruction of farmland. Millions of tonnes of soil blew away, some of the soil being carried as far as New York. The dust storms were called 'Black Blizzards'.

Winds which swirl in tight circles are called tornadoes or twisters. In 1931 a tornado in Minnesota lifted an 83 tonne train 25 metres into the air. When if fell, many of the passengers were killed.

Hurricanes can be up to 300 miles across. One of America's worst hurricanes occurred in 1900. Three thousand houses were destroyed in Galveston, Texas. Six thousand people were killed. An estimated two billion tonnes of water flooded the city.

Madness

The insistent cold Mistral wind of Southern France is reputed to drive people mad.

In Italy, the Scirocco is a stifling hot wind from the Sahara. It causes lethargy, insanity and suicide.

A 'simoom' is the Arabic name for a violent wind which raises maddening sandstorms in North Africa.

What to do if you're caught in a blizzard

Find shelter.

Don't move about or stamp your feet. This uses up energy. Frostbite is better than death!

Huddle together for warmth and don't risk going for help.

Stay awake. Don't go to sleep if you get drowsy. You may never wake up!

ICE AND SNOW

Snow rarely falls in warm climates. Since all the early civilisations grew up in warm southern climates, there is little mention of snow in documents which have survived from the ancient world. However experience from the recent past suggests that throughout history glaciers, avalanches, blizzards and hail storms have all caused many disasters. Avalanches have been particularly dangerous because they strike suddenly. Mountain communities throughout the world continue to suffer from avalanches to this day. Blizzards cover wider areas but are more dangerous to livestock left in the fields and to travellers caught between settlements.

There was a Little Ice Age from about 1550 to 1850 when rivers such as the Thames froze over every winter. Frost Fairs (annual markets) were held on the Thames ice until 1814, when the ice suddenly gave way and sent hundreds of fair-goers plunging to a watery doom.

Two types of avalanche

Dust avalanches of fresh, heavy snow slide down mountains at speeds of up to 200 mph. A surge of air pressure is created in front of the fast moving wall of snow which is almost as dangerous as the snow itself.

Ground avalanches of wet snow rarely travel more than 60 mph, but forces of up to 100 tons per square yard have been reported.

Ice wars

The Russians have often relied on ice and snow to repel invaders. In 1812 Napoleon's army of half a million men was reduced to just 50,000 by the harsh sub-zero temperatures of the Russian winter.

When Hannibal attacked Rome in 218 BC he took his army through the Alps. He lost 18,000 men and several war elephants through avalanches.

Ice was later used as a weapon in the Alps during the First World War. Avalanches were deliberately started to sweep away advancing troops. Eighty thousand soldiers died this way.

In 1930, five German glider pilots had to bale out during a vicious thunderstorm. They fell to earth as ice-covered human hailstones.

> **Major ice and snow disasters**
> 218 BC Alps, avalanches devastated Hannibal's
>   army, 18,000 died
> 1499 Alps, mercenary destroyed, 400 died
> 1888 Beheri, India, hailstones, 246 died
> 1812 Eastern Europe, Napoleon's army destroyed,
>   450,000 died
> 1906 Colorado avalanche wipes out town, 60 died
> 1910 Cascade Mnts. USA, avalanche, 118 died
> 1915-18 Alps, 80,000 soldiers killed
> 1932 Hunan, China, hailstones, 200 died
> 1951 Vals, Switzerland, buried villages, 240 died
> 1962 Huascaran, Peru, avalanche, 4,000 died
> 1970 Huascaran, Peru, 18,000 died

On 30 April 1888, hailstones as big as cricket balls fell in Northern India, killing 246 people and 1,600 sheep and goats.

On 18 July 1953, 60,000 ducks were killed by hailstones falling on Alberta, Canada.

The seven great Ice Ages were disastrous for many species of animal which failed to adapt to the freezing conditions. The woolly mammoth, however, was well adapted to cold. It was probably hunted to extinction by human beings. One mammoth was dug from the Siberian ice early this century. Deep-frozen for over 10,000 years, its meat was fresh enough to be eaten by explorers from the Royal Geographical Society.

Fog, smog and bolts from God

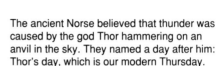

LIGHTNING

Disasters caused by lightning tend to be small scale. The focus of a lightning bolt is not much more than a single human being and its effect is limited unless it starts a fire. Lightning may travel at 100,000 miles per second on its journey between the clouds and the Earth.

The ancient Norse believed that thunder was caused by the god Thor hammering on an anvil in the sky. They named a day after him: Thor's day, which is our modern Thursday.

An American soldier was welded into his sleeping bag when lightning struck the zip in 1943.

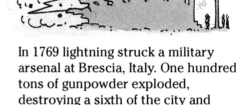

In 1769 lightning struck a military arsenal at Brescia, Italy. One hundred tons of gunpowder exploded, destroying a sixth of the city and wiping out three hundred inhabitants.

Between 1799 and 1815 lightning damaged 150 ships of the Royal Navy with 70 seamen killed and 130 seriously wounded.

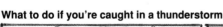

What to do if you're caught in a thunderstorm

If you're out in an open space such as a moorland, lie down under a plastic mac.

Don't stand under a tree - trees attract lightning.

A car's metal shell protects its passengers from lightning.

METEORITES

Like lightning, the damage done by meteorites is limited to a small area, unless they are very large or they start a fire.

Most meteorites are smaller than a grain of sand. But one weighing perhaps 70,000 tonnes hit Arizona about 50,000 years ago, leaving a huge crater still visible today.

A meteor which fell on China in 616 BC killed 10 men and broke several chariots.

On 30 June 1908, an object which may have been part of a comet exploded over Siberia. It destroyed over 8 million trees in an area of 2,000 square miles.

One theory about the extinction of the dinosaurs is that a huge meteorite hit the Earth about 65 million years ago raising dust clouds which blotted out the Sun. This made the weather too cold for dinosaur eggs to hatch properly.

SMOG AND FOG

Smog is caused by the effects of industrial pollution and vehicle exhausts on naturally occurring fog. It's quite a recent phenomenon. Fog has always caused problems for people.

In December 1952, 4,000 Londoners died of breathing problems during a coal-fire smog called a 'pea-souper' which lasted 5 days. This prompted the government to bring in the Clean Air Act which made London a smokeless zone.

Before radar was invented, fog caused great problems at sea. In 1914, the liner *Empress of Ireland* collided in dense fog with a coal ship off the Canadian coast. Many of the passengers were asleep at the time. The liner sank in just 15 minutes, carrying 1,012 souls to their panic-stricken deaths.

FAMINE

Ancient Man lived by hunting animals and gathering wild plants to eat. People moved on when the local food supplies ran out. When farming was developed about 8000 BC, people began to live in houses and the size of populations increased. It was then much harder to move away if war or natural disaster struck. Reliance on one or two main crops also increased the risk of famine. If the main crop failed there was little to eat in its stead. Crop failure regularly brought famine to Egypt and other early civilizations. The earliest written reference to a famine is in an Egyptian document of around 3500 BC. Together with war, famine remains the major cause of disaster to this day.

Major famine disasters	
3500 BC	Egypt, first recorded famine
436 BC	Rome, famine in the city
1235	London, bark eaten, 20,000 died
1333-37	China, Black Death, famine, 6 million died
1769	France, thousands died
1769-70	India, 13 million died
1790-92	India, 'Skull Famine', millions died
1800-50	China, four major famines, 45 million died
1846-47	Ireland, potato blight, 1,029,552 died
1932-34	USSR, collective farming failed, 5 million died
1967-70	Nigeria, social unrest and crop failure, one million died
1969-74	Sahel Desert, Africa, drought, 1 million died
1984-85	Ethiopia, drought and war, 5 million died

The Irish relied heavily on potatoes in the early nineteenth century. In 1845, a fungus disease called blight destroyed the crop, causing widespread famine during 1846-48. Over a million people died, and a million more emigrated to America.

Potato riot

The 1769 crop failure in France caused famine which wiped out one in twenty of the peasants, and helped set the scene for the later French Revolution.

In 1235, famine caused 20,000 deaths in London. People were reduced to eating grass and the bark of trees.

Pests

Locusts regularly caused famines in ancient Egypt.

Grasshoppers plagued the USA in the 1930s and '40s.

The rice crops of Asia are regularly attacked by Java sparrows.

African weaver birds sometimes form huge flocks up to 20 million strong which devastate crops.

Billions of French Guianian termites ate all that country's crops in the 1940s.

Sixty million mice destroyed crops in Bihar, India in 1899.

Up to 4 million Chinese starved to death between 1333 and 1337. The plague which then attacked the weakened, starving people spread by ship and overland caravans to the rest of the world. This plague was the Black Death.

Drought and famine affected Sudan, Ethiopia and Somalia in the 1960s, '70s and '80s. The deaths of perhaps 5 million Ethiopians in 1984-85 led to the formation of popular charitable efforts such as Band Aid, Live Aid and Comic Relief.

Famine has been recorded in India since around AD 900. The great famine of 1790-1792 was called the 'Doji Bara', or 'skull-famine', because the dead were too numerous to be buried. Only twenty years earlier, in 1769-1770, up to ten million died during a drought in Bihar.

Remedies for Spanish flu

Get very drunk.
Smear hot bacon fat on
your neck and chest.
Take a very cold bath.
Take a very hot bath.

The influenza virus produces a new strain every few years. Once in a while a new strain turns out to be a killer. So it was with Spanish flu, 1918-1919. World-wide, 20 million people died in just 120 days. Many different methods of avoiding infection were attempted.

PLAGUE

A disease which is always present in a population is called an endemic disease. Typhoid and cholera are endemic in poor countries without fresh water supplies. The young, the old and the weak are usually the most affected. But sometimes a specially dangerous disease threatens the lives of entire populations. Such diseases are called epidemics. The old word for an epidemic is a plague.

For 12 years from 1338 the Black Death struck Europe and Asia. Victims shivered and sweated, then huge black blobs appeared on their skin and they died in convulsive agony. The plague was carried by infected rats which flourished in the crowded dirty cities of that time. Some infected refugees from the cities were killed by frightened villagers, because they showed symptoms of the plague, such as sneezing. World-wide, 75 million died of the plague.

According to the Book of Exodus in the Bible a plague of boils struck the people and animals of Egypt around 1250 BC.

Leprosy was brought from the Middle East to Europe by the crusaders in the eleventh century. Leprosy was a major killer in the Middle Ages. To warn healthy people that they had the disease, lepers had to wear special clothes and signal their approach with a clapper or bell.

Malaria is spread by mosquitoes. It still kills up to two million people every year. Now largely confined to the tropics, it was once common in Europe.

From 1500, smallpox swept through Europe killing millions. Between 1700 and 1800, sixty million Europeans died of this disease. It was finally eradicated in 1977.

Yellow fever is another disease which is carried by mosquitoes. Death results from liver or heart failure. Between 1700 and 1900 huge epidemics spread from the tropics into America and Europe. It continues to strike. Between 1960 and 1962 an epidemic killed 20,000 Ethiopians.

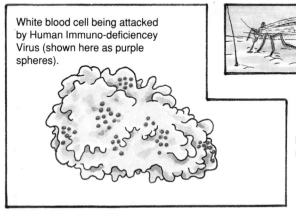

White blood cell being attacked by Human Immuno-deficiencey Virus (shown here as purple spheres).

Mosquito

Malaria microbes

Acquired **I**mmune **D**eficiency **S**yndrome (AIDS) is thought to have been endemic in Central Africa for centuries and may have been passed to humans by the bites of Green Monkeys. However, it only emerged as an international killer in the 1950s. It has now spread around the world, mostly by sexual contact. There are about 10 million cases now and by the year 2000 this may have risen to 40 million.

Heart disease is a modern plague. To avoid it in later life, most doctors advise you to:

eat less fat

not smoke

take regular exercise

1. Live a long way from potential targets such as cities.

2. Build a strong underground shelter. Fill it with stores.

3. Radioactivity should fall to fairly safe levels after about 60 years.

WAR

The use of force to resolve conflicts between groups of people is probably as old as the human race itself. It has been estimated that there have been only 300 years when no wars were recorded since written history began about 5,000 years ago. War has probably claimed more victims than any other type of disaster, especially since famine, fire and plague often follow in its wake.

During the Battle of Crécy, 1346, English bowman released up to 60,000 arrows a minute at the advancing French cavalry. One and a half thousand French knights were killed.

Approximately three-quarters of the male population of Britain died or were enslaved during the Roman Conquest, AD 43–84.

When the French army was passing through Poland on its way to Moscow in July 1812, 80,000 men died of, or were sick with, typhus.

Major war disasters
Since 1500 BC there have been at least 378 named wars. The estimated number of military deaths alone is more than 45 million.

The highest death toll caused by a single bomb occurred on 6th August 1945, when an atom bomb was dropped on Hiroshima, Japan, killing 140,000 people.

'Little Boy', the first atomic bomb

Brave but crazy

Lord Cardigan led the Charge of the Light Brigade in 1854 during the Crimean War. Six hundred and seven English cavalrymen armed only with swords charged Russian artillery positions. Four hundred and nine were killed. Lord Cardigan rode right through the enemy lines and back again without noticing the disaster. The buttoned woolly garment called a cardigan is named after him.

'General' George A. Custer led a force of 212 men against a much greater force of Sioux braves at Little Big Horn in June 1876. His entire force was killed.

Pyrrhus, the Greek commander at the Battle of Beneventum in 275 BC, was beaten by the Roman forces when one of his military elephants ran amuck and slaughtered many of his own troops.

Military expenditure during World War II is put at $1.5 trillion. This is more than all the other wars in history put together.

General Robert E. Lee thought his Confederate troops were invincible. After three days of suicidal attacks against fortified Union lines at Gettysburg, 1865, 7,500 of his men had died.

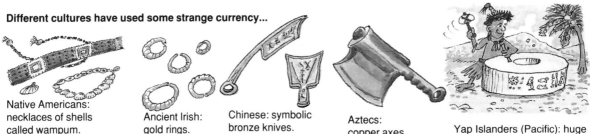

Different cultures have used some strange currency...

Native Americans: necklaces of shells called wampum.

Ancient Irish: gold rings.

Chinese: symbolic bronze knives.

Aztecs: copper axes.

Yap Islanders (Pacific): huge carved stones weighing up to half a ton.

FINANCIAL FOUL-UPS

Before money was invented, people traded by bartering. But this was often inconvenient. Travelling traders had to carry all their heavy goods with them. Metal money was first used about 600 BC by the Lydians of Asia Minor (now Turkey). Small pieces of gold or silver were stamped with a design or a king's head to show they contained a particular weight of precious metal. These 'coins' could then be exchanged for goods of an equal value.

Paper money was first used instead of metal coins in China during the reign of Kublai Khan (1215-1294). But paper money, cheques and share certificates only have value as long as people believe that these pieces of paper represent real wealth, because the paper they are written on has no value in itself. The system works as long as people believe in it. Sometimes for a variety of reasons, people stop believing. When that happens there is a financial crisis.

After losing the First World War, Germany was forced to pay reserves of gold to the victors. In the meantime the German banks continued to print paper money. But paper money is really only a promise to pay. If a government is bankrupt, its paper money becomes worthless. If the government has no other form of wealth, such as gold, to back up its paper money, the paper money eventually becomes worthless. Confidence in the German mark collapsed. In 1914, one US dollar was worth four marks. By 1924, it was worth four TRILLION marks. People took wages home in wheelbarrows. Inflation was so rapid that a cup of coffee could double in price between sips. Thousands of people faced starvation.

Children played in the streets with worthless banknotes.

In 1929 a few business failures led to unease and then to wholesale panic as other share prices fell on the Wall Street Stock Exchange in the USA. People queued overnight to retrieve money from their bank accounts. Banks ran out of money - 11,000 of them went bankrupt by 1933. Ruined bankers and business men committed suicide by jumping into rivers or out of tall buildings. The Wall Street Crash led to the Great Depression of the 1930s when there was massive unemployment in America and Europe.

Towards the end of the Roman Empire the government in Rome became desperate for money to pay its armies and public servants. More and more coins were produced. This caused massive inflation which weakened the Roman Empire still further.

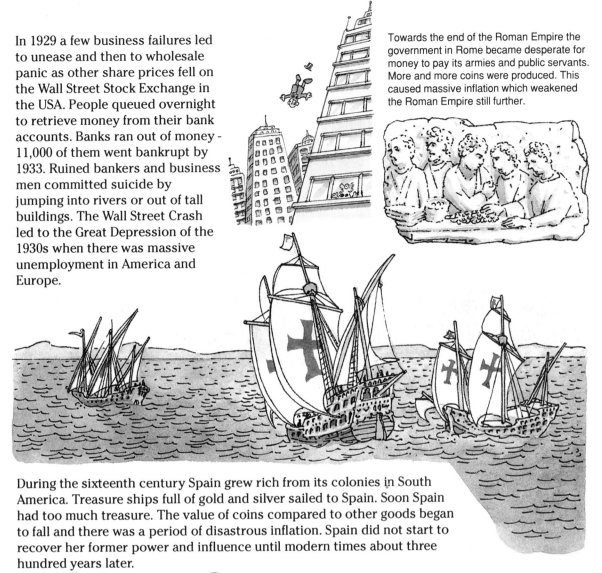

During the sixteenth century Spain grew rich from its colonies in South America. Treasure ships full of gold and silver sailed to Spain. Soon Spain had too much treasure. The value of coins compared to other goods began to fall and there was a period of disastrous inflation. Spain did not start to recover her former power and influence until modern times about three hundred years later.

In England in 1720 the South Sea Company which traded with South America appeared to be hugely profitable. There was a greedy scramble to buy shares in the company. Millions of pounds changed hands and the price of shares reached ridiculous heights. But buyers were being deceived by the company directors and the real value of the shares was far less. When no profits appeared, panic selling led to the collapse of these and other overpriced shares. Britain's entire economy was almost destroyed as the 'South Sea Bubble' burst.

In 1634 one Dutch merchant traded these items for a single rare tulip bulb:
two lasts of wheat
four lasts of rye
four fat oxen
eight fat swine
twelve fat sheep
two hogsheads of wine
four tuns of beer
two tuns of butter
a thousand pounds of cheese
a complete bed
a suit of clothes
a silver drinking-cup

In the 1630s Dutch tulips became very valuable. The Dutch economy became dependent on tulips. When the price of tulips collapsed there was a major financial disaster in Holland with mass poverty and suicides.

INDUSTRIAL DISASTERS

The Industrial Age is reckoned to have started in England around 1750 when steam and steel technology was first developed. Since that time industrial accidents have become more deadly as industry has used ever more dangerous chemicals and ever larger amounts of energy.

Although industrial disasters hit the headlines, more death and injury is caused by the small-scale accidents which happen every day.
Workers fall into vats of beer in breweries, composers go deaf, printers fall into printing presses...

Many industrial accidents start with explosions. These kill directly or cause leaks of poisonous chemicals. They can kill or injure people far away from the source of the accident. The effects of accidents in nuclear power plants have been felt thousands of miles away.

In 1986, a nuclear reactor exploded at the Chernobyl power station in the Ukraine. A toxic cloud of radioactive gas spread out over Europe. Eight thousand may have died from radiation sickness. This was the world's worst nuclear accident.

On 7 December 1917 the *Mont Blanc* was rammed by another ship in the harbour of Halifax, Nova Scotia. She was carrying explosives. The resulting blast killed 2,000 people.

In 1929, 1,000 people are thought to have died when a secret germ warfare factory blew up at Sverdlovsk in the former USSR. Deadly anthrax germs were spread over a large area.

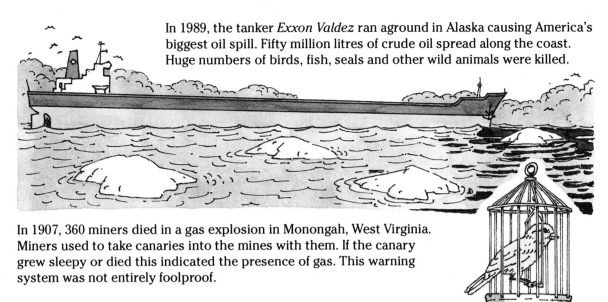

In 1989, the tanker *Exxon Valdez* ran aground in Alaska causing America's biggest oil spill. Fifty million litres of crude oil spread along the coast. Huge numbers of birds, fish, seals and other wild animals were killed.

In 1907, 360 miners died in a gas explosion in Monongah, West Virginia. Miners used to take canaries into the mines with them. If the canary grew sleepy or died this indicated the presence of gas. This warning system was not entirely foolproof.

In 1984 at Bhopal, India, a poisonous gas leaked from a storage tank at a factory which make batteries. At least 2,500 local people are recorded as dying from the poisonous, choking fumes. At least 500,000 more were injured but lived to file damage claims against the American factory owners, Union Carbide.

In the 1950s, a chemical plant at Minamata, Japan, emptied poisonous mercury compounds into the sea. At least 150 of the local population soon died from eating contaminated fish. Others are still suffering from brain damage.

Major industrial disasters
1866 Oaks colliery, England, explosions, 361 died
1907 Monongah Mine, West Virginia, explosion 360 died
1913 Senghenydd Colliery, Wales, explosion 439 died
1917 Halifax, Nova Scotia, explosion on a ship, 2,000 died
1947 Texas City Harbour, fire spreading to 50 oil tankers, 800 died
1953-93 Minamata, Japan, mercury leak, 300 died to date
1966 Aberfan, Wales, coal tip slide, 116 children died
1967 *Torrey Canyon*, oil tanker spillage, massive ecological damage to UK coast.
1976 Seveso Italy, chemical factory explosion, massive ecological damage
1979 Sverdlovsk, USSR, anthrax germ leak, 1000 died
1979 *Aegean Captain* and *Atlantic Empress*, two-tanker collision, world's biggest oilspill, 27 died
1984 Bhopal, India, chemical factory leak, 2,500 died
1986 Chernobyl, Ukraine, nuclear power explosion, 8,000 died
1989 Alaska, *Exxon Valdez* oil tanker spillage, massive ecological damage to coast

Flames from the 1944 Cleveland Ohio gas explosion rose 2,800 feet into the air. Pigeons fell to ground having been fully roasted in mid-air.

The safest place to sit

On the deck of a ship.

At the back of a train.

In the back passenger seat of a car.

At the back of an aeroplane.

TRANSPORT

One of the earliest descriptions of an accident involving transport is in the Old Testament. When pursuing the Israelites in their flight from Egypt, Pharaoh's chariots sank in the Red Sea.

But it was when transport became motorised that more transport accidents happened. The first, steam-driven, automobile crashed on its first run in 1769. Ships and trains made travel available to hundreds and sometimes thousands of people at a time.

The giant airships were filled with highly inflammable hydrogen gas. On 6 May 1937, the German airship liner *Hindenberg* burst into flames when landing in New Jersey. Static electrical sparks from a mooring mast had started the fire. Miraculously, out of 97 on board, only 33 died. This was the last of a number of fatal fires involving hydrogen airships.

The highest death toll in a single plane accident occurred in 1977 when two planes collided on the runway of Tenerife airport. Five hundred and eighty-three people died.

Major air disasters
1913 *LZ-18* German airship, first major air disaster, 28 died
1930 British R101 airship, explosion, 48 died
1937 *Hindenburg*, German airship, fire, 33 died
1974 Forest near Paris, Turkish airlines crash, 344 died
1977 Tenerife airport, runway collision, 583 died
1985 Mount Osutaka, Japan airline crash, 520 died
1988 Lockerbie, Pan Am terrorist bomb, 270 died
1989 Off Ireland, Air India terrorist bomb, 329 died

Major train disasters
1864 Shohola, Pennsylvania, head-on collision, 148 died
1879 Tay Bridge collapsed, Scotland, 75 died
1915 Troop train in collision with two other trains, Scotland, 227 died
1917 Troop train brake failure, Modane, France, 543 died
1944 Train collision, Salerno, Italy, 526 died
1981 Bridge collapsed, Bihar, India, 800 died
1989 Gas pipeline explosion, two trains passing, Siberia, 500 died

The first recorded death from a train accident occurred at the opening ceremony of the Liverpool to London line in 1830. An over-excited MP, William Huskisson, fell in front of *The Rocket*. His leg was severed.

In one of the world's worst train disasters, 543 soldiers died when the brakes failed on a troop train going down hill in France in 1917. It crashed on a bend having reached a speed of 100 mph.

The world's worst road disaster happened in the Salang Tunnel linking the USSR and Afghanistan in 1982. Two military convoys were involved. Possibly 2,000 people died from fumes and other injuries.

People were frightened by the speed and power of the first motor cars. In some countries the law insisted that a man with a red flag walk in front of every car.

On 7th May 1915, the US luxury liner *Lusitania* was sunk by a German U-boat. 1,198 lives were lost. Americans were outraged by this attack and in 1917 joined in the First World War against the Germans.

Thinking that the liner *Titanic* was unsinkable, some passengers held a snowball fight on deck with pieces of ice after their ship had collided with an iceberg. One thousand five hundred and three of the two thousand two hundred and seven passengers and crew perished when the *Titanic* sank.

Major ship disasters
1865 Mississippi river, *Sultana* steamer overloaded, 1,547 died
1849 Manchuria, Chinese troopship exploded, 6,000 died
1904 East River, New York, *General Slocum* ferry boat caught fire, 1,021 died
1912 North Atlantic, *Titanic* collides with iceberg, 1,503 died
1915 *Lusitania*, sunk by German submarine, 1,198 died
1954 Japan, *Taya Maru* ferry sunk by typhoon, over 1,000 died

It is estimated that Sunnynook, Canada is the safest place on Earth. It is far from any fault line so there is no danger of earthquake or volcano. Canada is not engaged in any wars. There is no danger of flooding, not much traffic so little danger of accidents, and there are modern health services to cope with disease. There's plenty of food so there is no danger of starvation. Central Canada does not suffer from hurricanes. The only danger is snow - and they're well prepared.

RESCUE AND PREVENTION

The damage caused by natural disasters can be reduced if people have some warning that a disaster is about to happen. These days there are various scientific methods of predicting natural disasters.

Man-made disasters should be more preventable than natural disasters, but regulations and safety devices often fail, and there is always the possibility of human error.

Once a disaster has happened, the work of rescue can stretch the resources of a country to the limit. Most countries now have rescue services which are kept in a state of readiness in case a disaster should occur. Even so the problems caused by a major disaster can be overwhelming.

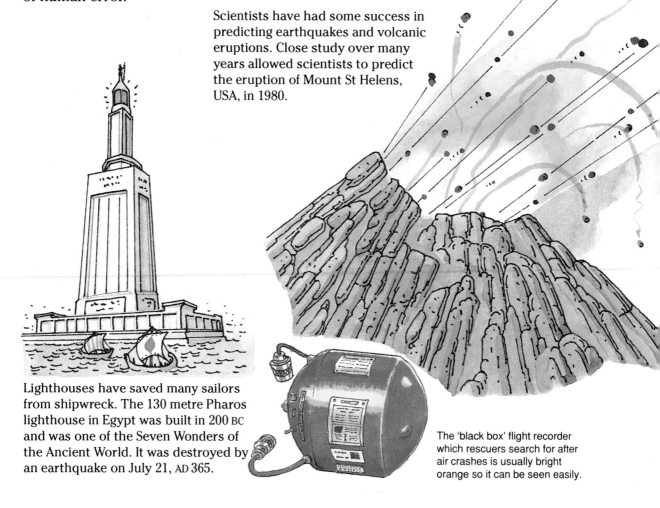

Scientists have had some success in predicting earthquakes and volcanic eruptions. Close study over many years allowed scientists to predict the eruption of Mount St Helens, USA, in 1980.

Lighthouses have saved many sailors from shipwreck. The 130 metre Pharos lighthouse in Egypt was built in 200 BC and was one of the Seven Wonders of the Ancient World. It was destroyed by an earthquake on July 21, AD 365.

The 'black box' flight recorder which rescuers search for after air crashes is usually bright orange so it can be seen easily.

Since the 1970s, hurricanes have been tracked by weather satellites so an early warning can be given about their paths. The practice of naming hurricanes was started by the Australian Clarence Wragg in the nineteenth century, who called them after people he didn't like.

Throughout the centuries, people have tried to stop hail damaging crops. The Greeks sacrificed animals and Italian peasants rang bells and hung out lucky charms.

Around 1900, European farmers tried firing blank charges from a 'hail cannon' to shatter hailstones before they fell.

Rescue vehicles

Fleets of ambulances are needed to evacuate victims.

Planes have been used to bomb lava flows in order to divert the course of lava away from towns.

The first fire engines were horse drawn vehicles owned by private insurance companies.

Mobile cranes and bulldozers are often needed to remove fallen masonry from the victims of earthquakes or explosions.

The hulls of lifeboats were once filled with ping-pong balls to reduce the danger of sinking.

Helicopters are useful after most disasters.

In Russia, planes drop cement powder onto clouds to precipitate rain and thus avoid both droughts and storms.

In Southern France and Canada, planes scoop water from the sea or the lakes to fight forest fires.

Fire-ships pump water directly from bodies of open water.

Avalanche rescue centres maintain sledges stocked with life-saving equipment, including 'sounding rods' - long probes for sticking into snow to search for bodies.

FUTURE DISASTERS

In the past, man-made disasters have been much less destructive than natural disasters, but in the future this may change. Environmental damage due to human activity, such as global warming, could result in disasters on a scale never seen before. And in the meantime, natural disasters like volcanoes, hurricanes and earthquakes will continue to happen. A fairly horrible history could turn into a very horrible future.

Ice Ages have occurred regularly for the last seven million years. The last one ended 10,000 years ago. The next one may be on its way.

The Norse believed that there would be three years of perpetual winter before Ragnarok, or Doomsday.

An estimated 100 billion meteorites strike the Earth's atmosphere every day. Most of them are small and burn up before hitting the surface. But a giant meteorite may have caused the extinction of the dinosaurs. Another giant may hit at any time.

Overpopulation is a present day disaster. The rate of increase in the world's population makes it likely that famines and wars will be even more destructive in the future.

Modern weapons systems are immensely powerful. There are more than enough nuclear weapons in the world to destroy all human life.

Careless use of agricultural genetic engineering may upset the world's ecological balance.

Deadly new microbes may escape from laboratories causing epidemics far worse than the plague or AIDS.

The temperature of the Earth's atmosphere may rise due to our use of fossil fuels. The ice caps could melt, causing sea levels to rise. Most of the world's major cities are built near the sea.

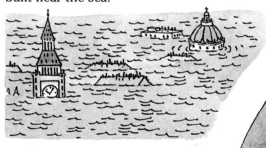

One disaster is certain to happen. In about 10 billion years the Sun will die. If the human race survives that long, it will have done very well indeed!

INDEX

First published in 1994 by
Watts Books
96 Leonard Street
London
EC2A 4RH

Paperback edition 1994

10 9 8 7 6 5 4 3 2 1

Franklin Watts Australia
14 Mars Road
Lane Cove
NSW 2060

© 1994 Lazy Summer Books Ltd
Illustrated by Lazy Summer Books Ltd

UK ISBN 0 7496 1187 1 (hardback)
UK ISBN 0 7496 1598 2 (paperback)

A CIP catalogue record for this book is
available from the British Library
Dewey Decimal Classification: 364

Printed in Belgium

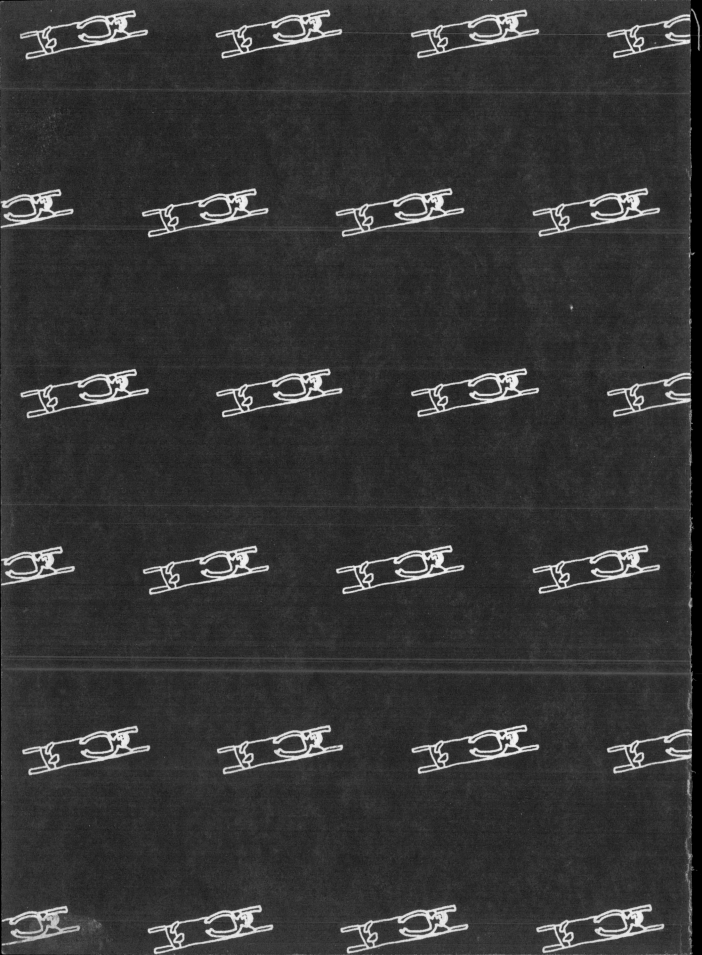